Teng Ying-chao, widow of Premier Chou En-lai, gives a warm welcome to the translator Nancy T. Lin and her husband Professor Dr. Li Yao-tzu in Peking in 1978.

IN QUEST

Poems of Chou En-lai

Vincenzo Labella

Pechino 1979

周恩来诗选

林同端英译

IN QUEST
Poems of Chou En-lai

Translated by Nancy T. Lin

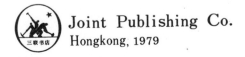

Joint Publishing Co.
Hongkong, 1979

Copyright @ 1979 by
Joint Publishing Co.
Hongkong Branch
9 Queen Victoria Street, Hongkong

First Published in January, 1979

Printed in Hongkong by
Chung Hua Book Co. Ltd.
Hongkong Printing Works
75 Pau Chung Street, Kowloon, Hongkong

Hardcover ISBN 962·04·0001·1
Paperback ISBN 962·04·0002·X

*To man's strivings
for a better world*

——*The translator*

Chou En-lai in 1919

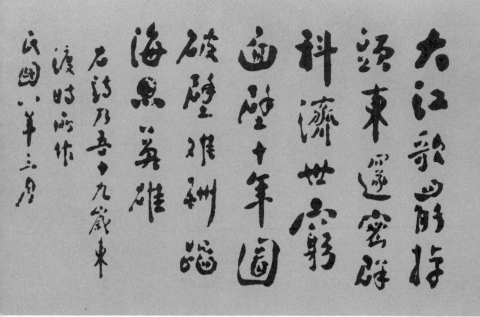

'Song of the Grand River Sung'
in the poet's own handwriting

CONTENTS

PUBLISHER'S NOTE

Chou En-lai's world-wide fame as a truly great statesman of New China has eclipsed his reputation in other fields. Few for instance knows that he wrote poetry. A number of poems he composed in his youthful days have been gathered from various sources and republished in the *People's Daily* and the *Poetry Journal* earlier the year. The acclaim by the reading public has been immediate and wide. For these poems, though less than a score, testify unmistakably to the practised skill of the author in the art of Chinese poetry. Above all, they reveal a highly delicate esthetic sense and sensibility that is in fact part of the makings of Chou the statesman.

Nancy T. Lin's English renderings of these poems, published here together with her perceptive preface, have captured the spirit of the Chinese original, combining a responsive interpretation with fluency of speech. A moving tribute to Chou En-lai, containing a brief account of his life written by Soong Ching Ling, is incorporated here with the permission of *China Reconstructs* as a background reading for the poems in general.

Nancy T. Lin (Lin Tung-tuan), graduate of Department of English, Southwestern Associated University, Kunming and M. A. in American literature, Mills College, California, has been back to China twice in the past three years. Her acquaintance with Chinese and American literature and her interest in the life and letters of present-day China have led her in recent years to taking translation of Chinese poetry as her chief avocation.

I

PREFACE

The poems that follow punctuate a journey—the journey of a youth in quest of a way out for his country, for man. The sorrow, the yearning, the groping, the despair, the struggle again, the widening of the horizon, the gleaming of light. Finally he comes upon what he terms as the Awakening, the road to take, the cause to fight for—in life and with death!

The poems reveal to us the poet in Chou En-lai. The ineffable quality of unaffected effusion that is the mark of a genuine poet—effusion born indeed of a sincerity of feeling and fineness of sensibility he fully evinces.

The poems take us to a glimpse, more intimate than any public utterance can provide, of Chou En-lai the man, his basic personality: the selfless devotion to ideals coupled with an ever-conscious concern for individual persons. What emerges before our eyes is the underlying fund of a broad, warm and scintillating humanity.

The poems are products of Chou's youthful days. But in them the matured Chou is pre-focussed in the round. They will go down the times as one more valued legacy keeping alive the uncontested love and respect China holds for that noble revolutionary and statesman who is her rightful pride.

林同端

(Nancy T. Lin)

May 4, 1978

Notes on a Spring Day

1914

I

A lookout from the suburb green:
Thickening fumes reek and reel.
Deer chases hot in the heartland;
Polang strikes close at heel.

II

Cherry blossoms flush over the paths,
Green willows shade the pier.
Twitter, twitter the swallows again:
Thoughts and yearnings through another year.

Written in 1914 when Yuan Shih-kai had betrayed the republican order which Sun Yat-sen sought to uphold. China was entering on the dismal period of lawless warlordism and intensified foreign aggression. Chou was 16 then, a student at the Nankai Middle School, Tientsin, and one of the organizers of the Ching Yeh (Devotion to Work) Society.

The poems, composed in the strict classical form of Five-word Short, were published in the 1st issue of the *Ching Yeh Review* which Chou was editing. They are the earliest poems of his known to us to date. They afford us a glimpse of the youthful heart and mind of the poet.

Deer chase: a traditional literary metaphor for war for dynastic rule and personal supremacy.

Polang strike: Chang Liang, a patriot of the state of Han in the period of the Warring States, sought to avenge his native land by an attempted assassination of the First Emperor of the Chin dynasty at Polang Sha (now Yuanyang County, Honan) 218 A.D. The term is used here to represent the revolt of the Chinese people against the warlords.

Thoughts on Seeing Peng-hsien off Home

Early 1916

I
There seemed a fated affinity
Though duckweed-like we met.
Nor was it accident that we
Bore the satchels both in Tientsin.
Lice—catching, you often stunned
Your friends with bold eloquence.
Crabs to wine now, we chew
Fondly over the bygone days.
Constant in weal and woe,
We mean to drink the gall.
The first to fight for our cause,
Dare we shun responsibilities?
Promise, I pray, that some day
When task done, we go back farming,
We'll surely rent a plot of ground
And as pairing neighbours let's live.

II

Songs of parting waft from the south beach
As the east wind urges travellers aboard.
In a twinkling, you'll be miles away.
All seems a dream—how soul consuming!
Stars fall apart to man's regret,
Clouds disperse for all we may care.
Stays but the pleasure of a recalled past—
Rich in mutual literary inspiration.

III

Of fellows joining in the race
You are the first to launch out.
Clumsy at hired tailoring, I admire
Your alacrity in face of giddy tides.
As broods of crows would roost under foliage,
So must the lone stork scour the skies.
Still, a unique regret lingers on
In the bosoms of friends at parting.

These three poems were published in the 4th issue of the *Ching Yeh Review*.

Peng-hsien: Chang Peng-hsien, a classmate of Chou's at Nankai and one of the co-organizers of the Ching Yeh Society. He was leaving Nankai for his home in Kirin Province in early 1916, pending his departure for Japan. These poems, the first in Seven-word Regular and the other two in Five-word Regular, demonstrate Chou's full mastery of the classical prosody. The noble resolve and the delicate sense of personal friendship as expressed here are traits Chou faithfully retained through the rest of his life.

Duckweed-like: "Like duckweed on the surface of water" is a literary metaphor for chance encounter or accidental meeting.

Lice-catching: derived from a Tsin dynasty story where a poor commoner-scholar Wang Meng, in his interview with Governor Huan Wen, discoursed eloquently upon state affairs while nonchalantly catching the lice on his coat in total disregard of other visitors. The term is indifferently used now to indicate uninhibited and fearless eloquence.

Drink the gall: a literary metaphor meaning "undergo all hardships to achieve one's aim."

Hired tailoring: odd job done for the sake of gaining a living.

5

Reply to Teacher Kao-ju's "Grieving Over Current Events"

September 1916

Whirls the Wind-and-Cloud
The dusky continent over.
All throughout the land
Sinks in a hushed gloom.
To top off the heartbreak,
Autumn is here again.
Chirp, chirp the crickets—
O, too much for the ear!

Kao-ju: Chang Kao-ju, teacher at Nankai and supporter of students' patriotic activities. With the death of Yuan Shih-kai, Chang Hsun, another warlord, summoned the Hsuchow Conference on September 28, 1916, in an attempt to form a warlord alliance of seven provinces and restore the feudal monarchy. Chang Kao-ju wrote a poem in lament over the event, declaring, "the life of the nation cut short by the hands of a few." Chou concurred with the piece shown above. Both poems were published in the 5th issue of the *Ching Yeh Review*. Chang, it may be noted, had joined the "poetic section" of the Ching Yeh Society at Chou's invitation.

Wind-and-Cloud: a literary expression for political cataclysm.

Song of the Grand River Sung

September 1917

Song of the Grand River sung,
I head resolute for the east,
Having vainly delved in all schools
For clues to a better world.
Ten years face to wall,
I *shall* make a break-through,
Or die an avowed rebel
Daring to tread the sea.

Written in September 1917 on the eve of the poet's departure for Japan. He was 19 then. In March 1919 when he was making preparations to return to China and take part in the movement against feudalism and imperialism, he recopied the poem as a memento for friends in Japan and as a "reminder for himself" of his earlier vow. The copy is now being kept in the Museum of Chinese History in Peking.

Song of the Grand River refers apparently to the poem by the Sung dynasty poet Su Tung-po in which he speaks of "the Grand River flows east, its waves having swept away heroes and all through the ages."

Face to wall: a literary term for intense solitary study and thinking.

Tread the sea: Lu Chung-lien, a champion against Chin hegemony in the period of the Warring States, declared that he would rather die by treading the East Sea than submit to the Chin invaders. The expression is used here to indicate the poet's resolve to die an avowed anti-imperialist fighter.

Arashiyama in the Rain
April 5, 1919

My second visit
To Arashiyama in the rain.
Blue pines line either bank,
Cherry trees interspersing.
A peak rises suddenly at the road's end.
A spring—flow of such jade green—
Winds its way among rocks, gleaming, glittering.
Drizzle rustling, mist thickening.
A beam of sunlight breaks through the clouds—
The more exquisitely enchanting!

Truths unnumbered
Implicit in the world's manifold.
The more search, the more haziness.
A chance glimpse of a spark in the haze—
The more indeed exquisitely enchanting!

Chou went to Japan in quest of truth, of the way out for China. In January 1919, he learned about Marxism from the semi-monthly *Studies on Social Problems*. He began expressing his new sense and feelings in his poems, now cast in free verse in place of the classical form. The present piece and the following three were written in April 1919 while still in Japan. They were published in the 1st issue of *Awakening*, a journal Chou founded soon after his return to China.

Arashiyama: a well-known scenic park in Kyoto.

Arashiyama after the Rain

April 5, 1919

Rain over,
The hill darkens with the clouds.
Dusk is approaching.
A backdrop of multitudinous green
Offers up a nimbus of cherry blossoms—
Delicately pink, tenderly sweet.
All soul-enchanting!
Beauty of nature, untouched by artfulness,
Unconstrained by man.
O, the plaster ornaments of religion, feudal
     ethics and outworn arts and letters,
The frustrating doctrines that are still
       being bandied about on so-called belief,
       sentiment and aesthetics!

A look in the distance
From heights ascended:
Hills melt in grey.
White clouds, part shaded,
Narrow down to a stripe.
A dozen electric lights glare from the dark

formless metropolis.

For a moment, a cry from the island people's hearts seems to break through the scene:

Elder statesmen, warlords, party bosses, capitalists, what from this, are you going to fall back on?

Maruyama Park

April 5, 1919

Cherry blossoms all over the park,
Brilliantly glowing;
Lights shining out on all sides;
Throngs of people chattering and clattering.
A drooping willow nestles by a small pond.
A young girl stands there all alone.
Which is the lovelier—
The cherry blossoms or the willow?
Quite forlorn, she speaks not a word.
And nobody seems to care.

Fourth Visit to Maruyama Park

April 9, 1919

My fourth visit here.
Uphill and over dale—
One riotous flood of fallen petals!
Nothing but green leaves on the branches,
With the solemn pines looking on.
Where are we to find
"The cherry blossoms,
Delicately pink, tenderly sweet?"

Lights out.
Fewer and fewer people.
Nine days in Kyoto
Has gained me a full draft of its bittersweet.
Bloom and decay,
Triumph and defeat,
Are the objective givens in this world of men.
Has there been indeed
All flower and spring,
Beauty of nature and unimpeded mental play?

The Indolence of Life-in-death

December 1919

Whiz! whiz! the northwest wind!
Winter has set in.
Going out, I hire a rickshaw.
The rickshaw man has a cotton padded coat on.
I, too, have a cotton padded coat on.
I feel the pinch of cold in spite of my coat.
He feels it an extra burden to keep his on.
He strips it off and covers my feet with it.
I thank him for being considerate.
He thanks me for accommodating him.

Co-existence with mutual benefit?
The sweating of men alive!
The indolence of life-in-death!

The May 4th Movement was on and China in the first flush of intellectual revolution. September 16, 1919 Chou founded the Awakening Society advocating "a fundamental remaking of man's social institution." The poem, recording an intimate personal experience, is a decisive pronouncement of Chou's against the old order of exploitation with a distinct Marxist orientation. It was published in the 1st issue of *Awakening*.

Bon Voyage to Li Yu-ju
with Remembrances to Shu-ti

June 8, 1920

An absence of three months
And how you have progressed!
Nien-chiang came the other day
Saying that you meant to go to England.
I thought you were only talking.
A couple of days later, Tan-wen told me
You were going to France.
I took it again as jesting.
Not many days had passed
When surprisingly enough
You came to bid me good-bye
And told me in person
That you were to go.
So, you are really going!

Shu-ti wrote me,
Quoting you as saying:
". . . I'm a person too.
I can provide myself by working.
Anyhow, I shan't be starving abroad!

You ought to know—
Happiness has to be sought;
Sitting pretty and waiting
Won't get you anywhere."

Then too your words to me at parting:
". . . buy a 4th class ticket,
Or take a 3rd class berth. . .
Off on a work-study basis.
In a year I'll be self-supporting,
Going in for applied chemistry and physics.
My wish and aim is—
Blaze a trail of freedom,
For women's material and spiritual independence,
Guard their inalienable rights."

There then is your spirit,
Your decision,
Your courage,
Your bubbling aspiration
Backed up by a will to fight!
From these shores,
You'll course through the East Sea,
The South Sea, the Red Sea and Mediterranean,
Whose waves and currents,

Surging and rolling far and on,
Will take you to the coast of France,
Home of liberty.

Once there,
Take up your tools,
Sweat away at your labor
And set a brilliant record.
Develop your skills,
Keep your innocence.

Coming back some day,
You'll unfurl the standard of freedom,
Strike up the song of independence.
You'll fight for women's rights,
Seek equality,
Plunge yourself into action.
You'll overthrow the out-dated ethics,
All by dint of a thought in your mind!

In Nanking!
There, you'll meet Shu-ti!
At the Hsiakuan Station,
By the Huangpu River,
I could see for you two
A trying moment of parting.

But aren't we in one world,
Why speak of separation!
Moreover, love spins on forever.
"The lotus root breaks but not the fibres."
Two months from now,
The New Continent will bear Shu-ti's foot prints.
Breakers of the Atlantic
Will keep your correspondance unbroken.
Like two wireless poles
Standing on opposite shores, east and west,
You'll join breaths through the space.

Three months from now,
On the wharf of Marseilles,
In the suburbs of Paris,
Maybe you and I shall meet.

Bon voyage, friend,
You are really going,
And capable of going too.
An absence of three months—
How you have progressed!

      —En-lai at the detention house of the local
        Investigation Bureau, Tientsin, 9. 6. 8.

Dear Yu-ju:

You are going away. Sorry I can't see you off. Let me send you a poem instead! I started composing it at 4:30 p.m. and actually succeeded finishing it by 6:30. In quality, this piece should rank middle-upper in my poetic works.

What do you think of it? Let Shu-an have a look at it when you see him in Nanking. Mail ships permitting, would you reply my piece with one of your "natural poesy?" Au revoir! Three months from now, perhaps we'll meet. Let's hope. Tien-an is going to send you a poem too.

En-lai   9. 6. 8.

On January 29, 1920, Chou was arrested by the Tientsin police for the leading part he took in the student demonstration against Sino-Japanese unequal treaties and demand for the freedom of assemblage etc. He was not released until July 17. On June 8, while still in detention, he wrote the above poem. The manuscript, secretely brought to Li Yu-ju then, is now being kept in the Historical Museum of Tientsin.

Li Yu-ju was a schoolmate of Teng Ying-chao (Mrs. Chou) at the Girls Normal School of Chihli. She visited Chou at the detention house before setting out for France on a work-study program. Shu-ti was Pan Shu-an, a class-mate of Chou's at Nankai, and Li's fiance; he went to U.S.A. in September 1920. Nien-chiang was Tao Shang-chao, arrested together with Chou; he went to France with Chou in November 1920 and later died in Paris. Tan-wen, i.e. Chao Kuang-chen, was a member of the Awakening Society. Tien-an, i.e. Ma Chun, chairman of the Tientsin Students Alliance, was arrested and detained together with Chou.

Parting in Life, Separation by Death

March 1922

From Shih-shan's letter to Nien-wu, I learn of the trea-
cherous murder of Comrade Huang Cheng-pin at the
hands of Chao Heng-ti and capitalists during the cotton
mill workers' strike in Changsha. For a while, trains of
thoughts and memories of the comrades in the struggle
come crowding in upon me. This poem, prompted by
the occasion, is an expression of my resolve and its
sharing with friends.

A heroic death.
A wretched life.
Clinging fondly to life in dread of death—
Is it not better to die a weighty death
That makes light of life!

Parted in life or separated by death—
The worst that could happen to men.
Parted—in sorrow, in anguish,
Dead—for naught that counts—
Is it not better to bid a farewell that inspires!

No sowing done,
No reaping possible.
Hankering for the blooms of communism
But not sowing the seeds of revolution,
Dreaming of Red Flags flying triumphant
Without consecrating them with blood:
Such a cheap gain—could there ever be?

Sit and talk—
Better rise and act!
They that cling to life
Will wail over partings,
Will let life or death lead them by the nose.

They will never understand
A farewell that inspires,
A soul-stirring farewell.
Hope resides in yourself and no one else.
The way of life or death lies open to all.
Fly towards light—
All's up to you!
So take up your hoes,
Open up the untilled land,
Seeds strewn among men,
Blood watering the earth.

Partings have always been.

More farewells are yet to come.
See life and death steadily,
And see both through:
Strive and make the best of your life,
Strive and make the best of your death.
What of it if it comes to bidding farewell?

Huang Cheng-pin: a native of Changteh, Hunan; joined the Awakening Society in 1919 while a student in Tientsin; active in organizing labor unions in Changsha, for which he was arrested several times; leader of the strike by the workers at Changsha's First Cotton Mill in January 1922; arrested January 16 and shot on the following morning.

The poem was written in March 1922 when Chou was in Germany busily organizing the European branch of the Communist Party of China. In a letter to friends in China, Chou spoke of the poem as an act of resolve in memory of Huang's death. "The news of his death has thoroughly strengthened my commitment to communism . . . I believe I shall prove worthy of my dead friend."

In June, 1922, under Chou's leadership, the Communist Party of Chinese Youth in Europe came into existence in Paris, and was renamed in winter as the European Branch of the League of Chinese Communist Youth with Chou as its Secretary.

In Memory of Premier Chou En-lai

Soong Ching Ling

When our Premier Chou En-lai died a year ago, messages of condolence from all over the world fell like heavy snowflakes on Peking, merging with the tears that engulfed China in shared sorrow over this gigantic loss.

From working class revolutionaries everywhere came tributes to his great services to the cause of the Chinese people's liberation and the cause of communism, his consistent defense and faithful, effective application of Marxism-Leninism-Mao Tsetung Thought.

Messages from governments spoke of him as a remarkable statesman of our time. With particular warmth, many from the third world hailed him as a fellow fighter in their own cause, who in a great many ways encouraged and helped their self-reliant struggle and development.

Countries want independence, nations want liberation, peoples want revolution. Wherever this irresistible tide of our times surges high, there Premier Chou is remembered as a friend in need, and in deed.

Always a patriot, always an internationalist, Chou En-lai was a complete proletarian revolutionary. Beginning his political activity in the patriotic anti-imperialist, anti-feudal awakening of the May 4 Movement of 1919, he came quickly to Marxism and propagated it among the Chinese students and workers abroad. He joined the Communist Party of China in 1922.

Returning to China in the period of the First Revolutionary Civil War of 1924—27, when the Chinese Communist Party entered into revolutionary cooperation with the Kuomintang founded and led by Sun Yat-sen, he became political director of the Whampoa Military Academy and helped create a vigorous armed force for the war against imperialist-backed, feudal, reactionary northern warlords. There I first met him in the mid-1920s, as a young but already seasoned and versatile leader, firm and clear-cut in his commitment to revolution. Shortly afterwards, in Shanghai he led the workers' uprising which heroically wrested that great city from warlord hands.

But Chiang Kai-shek, backed by all the imperialist and feudal forces, which feared and hated the revolution, then betrayed the cause of Sun Yat-sen, betrayed the united front of the time, turned on the people, massacred the workers and peasants, and became the biggest reactionary comprador warlord of all.

Chou En-lai was one of those who, uncowed by the murderous white terror, never stopped fighting but proceeded at once to organize the people's counterblow. With Comrades Chu Teh, Ho Lung, Chen Yi and others he led the Nanchang Uprising of August 1, 1927 whose forces joined with those of the Autumn Harvest Uprising led by Chairman Mao. The Nanchang Uprising fired the first gun against the Kuomintang reactionaries. Today, August First is China's Army Day.

In the course of the heroic and world-renowned Long March, of which he was one of the political and military organizers, Chou En-lai gave his full support to the crucial decision of the 1935 Tsunyi Meeting which established Chairman Mao's leadership in both Party and army and so put the Chinese revolution on its sure road to success. For decades thereafter, he was Chairman Mao's constant aide and comrade-in-arms, the day-to-day executive of his revolutionary line in struggles both domestic and international.

After the Long March triumphed, his capabilities were outstandingly demonstrated in the peaceful settlement of the Sian Incident* of December 1936. In consequence, the united front against the Japanese imperialist invaders was built and defended, and China's continued existence as a nation was achieved in 1945 after eight years of war.

To expose China's reactionaries in struggle in the form of negotiations was one of the arduous and complex tasks in those years, and I saw how well Chou En-lai shouldered it on behalf of the Party and people. In Chungking in the early 1940s peril constantly dogged his steps, but when he came to see me in connection with my work, he was always fearless and confident. When the war with Japan drew toward its end, his suggestions helped me to re-orient the work of the China Defense League to that of the China Welfare Fund (now Institute) in the new situation. Setting itself up in Shanghai, which in 1945-49 was under Kuomintang control, it initiated various projects of interim benefit to the working people while doing its utmost, by medical and other material aid, to channel help to the liberated areas that fought to bring full emancipation to our whole country and people.

The Party, its army and the united front were the weapons of victory in the Chinese revolution—and to the forging of each of these, Chou En-lai made his lasting contribution.

After World War II he fought and worked with equal loyalty, courage, tirelessness and skill. In the complex period of internal negotiations in 1945-46, in the decisive all-out armed struggle of 1947-49, and in the clarion proclamation of the People's Republic of China that marked the final throwing-off by the Chinese people of the three crushing burdens—imperialism, feudalism and bureaucrat-capitalism— he was at Chairman Mao's side.

In 1949 Chou En-lai became the premier of our new state, and continued so for 26 years, till the end of his life. He stood firmly with Chairman Mao against all opportunists and deviations, Right or "Left" in the multiple struggles of line within the Chinese Communist Party, in battling revisionism in the international communist movement, and in the steering of the Great Proletarian Cultural Revolution to overcome the threat of revisionism at home.

He was Chairman Mao's chief lieutenant in the building of the people's state power, the repairing of the internal ravages of war, the help to our neighbor Korea to repel U.S. imperialist invasion and defend our own borders, the successive transformations of our agriculture from land reform to cooperatives to communes and the building, on the basis of this progress, of China's industry. Under his premiership, China's economy forged ahead, her finances were well-balanced, foreign trade expanded and the people's livelihood markedly improved.

The economic policy he helped conduct is one adapted to a developing country, with a proper balance between centralization and local initiative, with the promotion of small industries in the rural communes, and with emphasis on agricultural development as the road to rapid and well-founded industrialization. It provides a contrast to the course taken in the Soviet Union, where agriculture and light industry are always in crisis, heavy industry is stressed in isolation, and the gap between workers and farmers has widened instead of narrowing. Another key feature Premier Chou helped build in China's economic policy is self-reliance, combined with readiness to learn all that is of use to us from foreign advances in science and technology. And a year before his death, he reiterated from the rostrum of the Fourth National People's Congress Chairman Mao's great plan of transforming China, which up to the middle of this century was so poor, backward and oppressed, into a great socialist country whose modern agriculture, modern industry, modern national defense, modern science and technology would be in the world's front ranks by this century's end. In this vast task of continuing socialist revolution and construction, we are now all engaged.

Premier Chou too was incessantly active in China's international affairs on the Party, government and people-to-people level. He traveled to a score of countries, talked with thousands of visitors to China, sent out many friendship delegations and was an architect of the famous Five Principles of Peaceful Coexistence. At the Geneva Conference of 1954 he waged diplomatic struggles to ensure to the peoples of Indochina the fruits of their heroic anti-colonial fight. At the Bandung Conference of 1955 his persistent stress on agreement on common basic interests and on shelving secondary differences helped unite what we now know as the third world—a bastion against imperialism, social imperialism and superpower hegemonism. In 1961 in Moscow he publicly defied the revisionist Soviet misleaders' attempt to outlaw and destroy Albania and pervert the then socialist camp and the world communist movement into a tool of their own betrayal of revolution. On his return, he was met at the airport by Chairman Mao whose instructions he had unwaveringly followed. Thus the seeds of genuine Marxism-Leninism were helped to sprout anew in the world.

In the sphere of diplomatic relations, Premier Chou carried out with great virtuosity Chairman Mao's policy of broadening to the utmost extent, and with no sacrifice of principle, the equal international links of China as a state—with a view first of all of overcoming barriers to the friendship among the peoples. One such success was the signing of the Shanghai Communique with U.S. President Richard Nixon in 1972. Another was the restoration of long-broken diplomatic relations with Japan. These achievements breached the imperialist policy of political and economic blockade of the People's Republic of China, and were helpful to understanding among peoples.

Here I would like to mention the warm encouragement

he always gave to our magazine *China Reconstructs* which is devoted to helping readers abroad to know and understand the new China.

A True Communist in his personal behavior and style, as well as in political action, Premier Chou lived simply and modestly, always accessible, always among the masses of working people as one of themselves. His food was plain —in the Red Army of old, in the economically difficult early 1960s and at all other times—he ate only what was readily available to all. He wore his clothes until they were threadbare or patched. At work he generally took canteen meals with his assistants including the most junior, often with his driver or, when traveling, with the crew of his plane, and in conversation both educated them and sought their opinion. So he was loved and appreciated by all around him, especially the young, who recall these contacts with tear-filled eyes.

Premier Chou kept himself closely informed about the people's livelihood, for which he showed incessant and deep concern. When a severe earthquake hit Hsingtai prefecture, Hopei province, in 1966 he dashed there while the area was still heaving with aftershocks to supervise relief and encourage the people to overcome the disaster. To an old man weeping inconsolably among the ruins of his home, he said, "Just consider me as your son." Thus he gave courage to all and moved beyond words those who heard him.

It is as a true Communist in every fiber of his being, as well as a communist statesman, that Chou En-lai will be forever remembered by the people. Upon the news of his death, hundreds of thousands of men, women and children in Peking flocked spontaneously to Tien An Men Square, covering it with flowers and wreaths. And in huge numbers they came to Chinese embassies and missions around the globe to mourn and honor him.

His entire life from his early student days before the 1920s until his heart stopped beating on January 8, 1976, was wholly devoted to the welfare of the people. His dying wish was that his ashes be scattered from the air over China's mountains and rivers. He is mingled with the people forever, in the earth they till, in the air they breathe.

Now, after the overthrow of the "gang of four", pretenders to power who were in every respect his opposites, and rallying around the Central Committee headed by Chairman Hua Kuo-feng, we once more pay tribute to Premier Chou. This gallant, tireless, intrepid and warmhearted fighter and worker who is loved by the people because he loved them, who was able to defeat all enemies and to unite all who could be united in the forward march, will be an example to us forever.

(From *China Reconstructs*, April 1977)

* Under the influence of the Chinese Red Army and the people's anti-Japanese movement, the Kuomintang's North-eastern Army headed by Chang Hsueh-liang and the Kuomintang's 17th Route Army headed by Yang Hu-cheng agreed to the anti-Japanese national united front proposed by the Communist Party of China and demanded that Chiang Kai-shek unite with the Communist Party to resist Japan. He refused, became still more active in his military preparations for the suppression of the Communists and massacred young people in Sian who were anti-Japanese. Chang Hsueh-liang and Yang Hu-cheng took joint actions and arrested Chiang Kai-shek. This was the famous Sian Incident of December 12, 1936. He was forced to accept the terms of unity with the Communist Party and resistance to Japan, and was then set free to return to Nanking.

Appendix:

Chinese Originals
of the Poems

春 日 偶 成 （二首）
一九一四年

极目青郊外，
烟霾布正浓。
中原方逐鹿，
博浪踵相踪。

樱花红陌上，
柳叶绿池边。
燕子声声里，
相思又一年。

送蓬仙兄返里有感（三首）
一九一六年

相逢萍水亦前缘，
负笈津门岂偶然。
扪虱倾谈惊四座，
持螯下酒话当年。
险夷不变应尝胆，
道义争担敢息肩。
待得归农功满日，
他年预卜买邻钱。

东风催异客，
南浦唱骊歌。
转眼人千里，
消魂梦一柯。
星离成恨事，

云散奈愁何。
欣喜前尘影，
因缘文字多。

同侪争疾走，
君独著先鞭。
作嫁怜侬拙，
急流让尔贤。
群鸦恋晚树，
孤雁入寥天。
惟有交游旧，
临歧意怅然。

次皞如夫子伤时事原韵
一九一六年

茫茫大陆起风云，
举国昏沉岂足云；
最是伤心秋又到，
虫声唧唧不堪闻。

无　　题
一九一七年九月

大江歌罢掉头东，
邃密群科济世穷；
面壁十年图破壁，
难酬蹈海亦英雄。

雨中岚山 —— 日本京都
一九一九年四月五日

雨中二次游岚山，
两岸苍松，夹着几株樱。
到尽处突见一山高，
流出泉水绿如许，绕石照人。
潇潇雨，雾濛浓；
一线阳光穿云出，愈见姣妍。
人间的万象真理，愈求愈模糊；
——模糊中偶然见到一点光明，真愈觉姣妍。

雨 后 岚 山
一九一九年四月五日

山中雨过云愈暗，
渐近黄昏；
万绿中拥出一丛樱，
淡红娇嫩，惹得人心醉。
自然美，不假人工；
不受人拘束。
想起那宗教，礼法，旧文艺，……
　　粉饰的东西，
还在那讲什么信仰，情感，
　　美观……的制人学说。

登高远望，
青山渺渺，
被遮掩的白云如带；
十数电光，射出那渺茫黑暗的城市。

44

此刻岛民心理，仿佛从情景中呼出：
元老，军阀，党阀，资本家，……
　　从此后"将何所恃"？

游日本京都园山公园
一九一九年四月五日

满园樱花灿烂；
灯光四照；
人声嘈杂。
小池边杨柳依依，
孤单单站着一个女子。
樱花杨柳，哪个可爱？
冷清清不言不语，
可没有人来问他。

四次游园山公园
一九一九年四月九日

四次来游，
满山满谷的"落英缤纷"；
树上只剩得青松与绿叶，
更何处寻那"淡红娇嫩"的"樱"！

灯火熄，游人渐渐稀，
我九天西京炎凉饱看；
想人世成败繁枯，都是客观的现象，
何曾开芳草春花，自然的美，无碍着的心

死人的享福

一九一九年十二月

西北风呼呼响，
冬天到了。
出门雇辆人力车，
车夫身上穿件棉袍，
我身上也穿件棉袍。
我穿着嫌冷，
他穿着却嫌累赘；
脱下来放在我的脚上，
我感谢他爱我，
他谢谢我助他便他。
共同生活？
活人的劳动！死人的享福！

别李愚如并示述弟

三个月没见你，
　进步的这般快了。
前些日子念强来说，
　你要往英，
　　我以为不过说说。
过几天丹文又来说，
　你要往法，
　　我也以为不过说说。
那知不几天，
　你来别我；
　当面告诉我，
　　你能去了。

你竟去了。

述弟来信告诉我，
　说你给他去的信道：
　　"……况且我是个人，
　　可以做工自给的；
　无论如何，
　　总不至饿死他乡！
　你要知道！
　　幸福是要自己去找；
　　株守相等，
　　是没有得到一日的。……"

　你别时也同我说：
　　"……买四等票，
　　坐三等舱。……
　　……勤工俭学去；
　　念一年书后，
　　工读自助。
　　……研究实用理化；
　　本我的志趣，
　　　辟我们女子的生计独立，精神
　　　　独立的自由径路；
　　　　保我们女子的人权天赋。……"

　念你的精神，
　　你的决心，
　　你的勇敢，
　兴勃勃的向上，
　　全凭你的奋斗壮胆。

47

出国去，
　　走东海、南海、红海、地中海，
一处处的浪卷涛涌，
　　奔腾浩瀚，
　　送你到那自由故乡的法兰西海岸。
到那里，
　　举起工具，
　　　出你的劳动汗；
　　　造你的成绩灿烂。
　　磨练你的才干；
　　保你天真烂漫。
他日归来，
　　扯开自由旗；
　　唱起独立歌。
　　争女权，
　　　求平等，
　　　　来到社会实验。
　　推翻旧伦理，
　　　全凭你这心头一念。

过南京，
　　见着述弟；
想象中下关车站，
　　　黄浦江畔，
　　一刹那的别离难。
同在世界上，
　　说什么分散。
何况情意绵绵，
　　"藕断丝不断"。
两月后，

新大陆又见了述弟的足迹。
大西洋的波澜，
　　流不断你们的书翰；
两个无线电杆，
　　矗立在东西两岸，
　　　气通霄汉。
三月后，
　马赛海岸，
　　巴黎郊外，
　　　我或者能把你看。

行行珍重！
你竟去了。
你能去了。
三个月没见你，
　进步的这般快了。

——九、六、八下午恩来作于
天津地方检察厅看守所

愚如：

　　你走了，不能送你，我做首诗送你吧！今天我从下午四点钟做起，做到六点半钟，居然成功了。这首诗的成绩，在我的诗集里，要算是"上中"了。

　　你看看怎样？到南京请给述庵看看！海船无到，你能本着"天籁"和我一首吗？

　　别了！三个月后，或者能见着，希望了。

　　天安也有一首诗送你！

恩来　九、六、八、

生 别 死 离
一九二二年

……知道黄君正品因长沙纱厂工人罢工事，遭了赵恒惕同资本家的诱杀。一时百感交集，更念及当时的同志，遂作此篇，用表吾意所向，兼示诸友。

壮烈的死，
苟且的生。
贪生怕死，
何如重死轻生！

生别死离，
　　最是难堪事。
别了，牵肠挂肚；
死了，毫无轻重，
　　何如作个感人的永别！

没有耕耘，
　　哪来收获？
没播革命的种子，
　　却盼共产花开！
梦想赤色的旗儿飞扬，
　　却不用血来染他，
　　天下哪有这类便宜事？

坐着谈，
　　何如起来行！
贪生的人
　　也悲伤别离，
　　也随着死生，

只是他们却识不透这感人的永别，
　　永别的感人。

不用希望人家了！
生死的路，
　　已放在各人前边，
飞向光明，
　　尽由着你！
举起那黑铁的锄儿，
　　开辟那未耕耘的土地；
种子散在人间，
　　血儿滴在地上。

本是别离的，
　　以后更会永别！
生死参透了，
　　努力为生，
　　还要努力为死，
　　便永别了又算甚么？